A Little Book of Virtues

DIMENSIONS
FOR LIVING
NASHVILLE

A Little Book of Virtues

This book is printed on recycled, acid-free paper.

ISBN 0-687-01600-2

Credits appear on page 48.

Printed in Hong Kong

This book was given to

by

on

Faith

Faith is the substance
of things
hoped for, the evidence of
things not seen.

Hebrews 11:1 KJV

Whatever you ask for
in prayer
with faith,
you will receive.

Matthew 21:22 NRSV

Let nothing disturb thee,
Nothing affright thee;
All things are passing;
God never changeth.

Saint Teresa

If you have faith as small as a mustard seed, you can say to this mountain, "Move from here to there" and it will move. Nothing will be impossible for you.

Matthew 17:20 NIV

Love

If instead of a gem, or
even a flower, we should
cast the gift
of a loving thought
into the heart of a friend,
that would be giving as
the angels give.

George MacDonald

For God so loved the world,
that he gave his only begotten
Son, that whosoever believeth
in him should not perish,
but have everlasting life.

John 3:16 KJV

Be on your guard;
stand firm in the faith;
be men of courage; be strong.
Do everything in love.

1 Corinthians 16:13-14 NIV

The fruit of the Spirit is
love, joy, peace, longsuffering,
gentleness, goodness, faith,
meekness, temperance: against
such there is no law.

Galatians 5:22-23 KJV

Loyalty

Know therefore that the
LORD your God is God,
the faithful God
who maintains
covenant loyalty with
those who love him and
keep his commandments.

Deuteronomy 7:9 NRSV

Do not let loyalty
and faithfulness forsake you;
bind them around your neck,
write them on the tablet of
your heart.

Proverbs 3:3 NRSV

Give us courage and strength to persevere. . . . Spare to us our friends and soften to us our enemies. Give us the strength to encounter that which is to come, that we may be brave in peril, constant in tribulation, temperate in wrath and in all changes of fortune, and down to the gates of death loyal and loving to one another.

Robert Louis Stevenson

You must
worship no other gods,
but only Jehovah,
for he is a God who claims
absolute loyalty and exclusive
devotion.

Exodus 34:14 TLB

Courage

Wait on the LORD:
be of good courage,
and he shall strengthen
thine heart: wait,
I say, on the
LORD.

Psalm 27:14 KJV

For I am persuaded,
that neither death, nor life, nor
angels, nor principalities, nor
powers, nor things present,
nor things to come, nor height,
nor depth, nor any other creature,
shall be able to separate us
from the love of God, which is
in Christ Jesus
our Lord.

Romans 8:38-39 KJV

I know . . .

In the darkest night of the year,
When the stars have all gone out,
That courage is better than fear,
That faith is truer than doubt.

Washington Gladden

Say not, "Too poor,"
but freely give;
Sigh not, "Too weak,"
but boldly try;
You never can begin
to live
Until you dare to die.

"Doors of Daring"
Henry van Dyke

Prudence

A prudent man
overlooks an
insult.

Proverbs 12:16 NIV

In conversation
be sincere:Keep conscience
as the noon-tide clear;
Think how all-seeing God
thy ways
And all thy secret
thought surveys.

"Awake My Soul"
Thomas Ken

Keep
sound wisdom and
discretion:
so shall they be life unto
thy soul, and grace to thy neck.

Proverbs 3:21-22 KJV

Lord,
I my vows to Thee renew;
Disperse my sins as morning dew;
Guard my first springs
of thought and will,
And with thyself my spirit fill.

"Awake My Soul"
Thomas Ken

Humility

God
resisteth the proud,
and giveth grace
to the humble.

1 Peter 5:5*b* KJV

Endeavor to be always patient of the faults and imperfections of others; for thou hast many faults and imperfections of thine own that require forbearance.

Thomas à Kempis

There is none like the
LORD our God
in heaven or on earth,
who sets his throne so high
but deigns to
look down so low.

Psalm 113:5-6 NEB

Take my yoke upon you,
and learn of me;
for I am meek and
lowly in heart: and ye
shall find rest unto
your souls.

Matthew 11:29 KJV

Trustworthiness

On the good ground
are they, which in an honest
and good heart, having heard
the word, keep it, and bring
forth fruit with patience.

Luke 8:15 KJV

Truth is the trial of itself,
And needs no other touch;
And purer than the
purest gold,
Refine it ne'er
so much.

Ben Jonson

Finally, beloved,
whatever is true, whatever is
honorable, whatever is just,
whatever is pure, whatever
is pleasing, whatever is
commendable, if there is any
excellence and if
there is anything worthy
of praise,
think about these things.

Philippians 4:8 NRSV

[Truth]
is the warrant of the word,
That yields
a scent so sweet,
As gives a power to faith
to tread
All falsehood under feet.

Ben Jonson

Temperance

Add to your faith virtue;
and to virtue knowledge;
and to knowledge temperance;
and to temperance patience;
and to patience godliness;
and to godliness brotherly
kindness; and to brotherly
kindness charity.

2 Peter 1:5-7 KJV

Jesus calls
us from the worship,
Of the vain world's golden store
From each idol that
would keep us, Saying,
"Christian, love me more."

"Jesus Calls Us"
Cecil Frances Alexander

When men
talk too much,
sin is never far away.

Proverbs 10:19 NEB

Our determination
to imitate Christ
should be such that we
have no time for
other matters.

Erasmus

In your hearts
set apart Christ as Lord.
Always be prepared
to give an answer to everyone
who asks you to give
the reason for the hope
you have. But do this
with gentleness and
respect.

1 Peter 3:15 NIV

Pay to all what is due them—taxes to whom taxes are due, revenue to whom revenue is due, respect to whom respect is due, honor to whom honor is due.

Romans 13:7 NRSV

Each of you, . . . should love his wife as himself, and a wife should respect her husband.

Ephesians 5:33 NRSV

O Lord, give us more charity, more self-denial, more likeness to you. Teach us to sacrifice our comforts to others and our likings for the sake of doing good. Make us kindly in thought, gentle in word, generous in deed. Teach us that it is better to give than to receive, better to forget ourselves than to put ourselves forward, better to minister than to be ministered unto. And to you, the God of Love, be all glory and praise, now and for ever.

Henry Alford

Justice

I know
thy justice is thyself;
I know, Just God, thy
very self is mercy too;
If not to thee, where,
whither shall I go?

Francis Quarles

To do justice
and judgment is more
acceptable to the LORD than
sacrifice.

Proverbs 21:3 KJV

For the LORD
is righteous, he loves justice;
upright men will see his face.

Psalm 11:7 NIV

To be trusted
is a greater compliment
than to be loved.

George MacDonald

Hope

Faith goes up the stairs that love has made and looks out of the windows which hope has opened.

C. H. Spurgeon

Blessed is the man
that trusteth in the LORD,
and whose hope the LORD is.
For he shall be as a tree
planted by the waters.

Jeremiah 17:7-8 KJV

It is good that a man should both hope and quietly wait for the salvation of the LORD.

Lamentations 3:26 KJV

Credits

Book design by Thelma Whitworth
Borders and decos from Aridi Computer Graphics, Inc. and the type font *Zapf Dingbats*.